A GIFT FOR:

_ _ _ _ _ _

FROM:

_ _ _ _ _ _

Hallmark

COPYRIGHT © 2016 HALLMARK LICENSING, LLC

PUBLISHED BY HALLMARK GIFT BOOKS,
A DIVISION OF HALLMARK CARDS, INC.,
KANSAS CITY, MO 64141
VISIT US ON THE WEB AT HALLMARK.COM.

EDITORIAL DIRECTOR: DELIA BERRIGAN
EDITOR: KARA GOODIER
ART DIRECTOR: CHRIS OPHEIM
DESIGNER: SCOTT SWANSON
PRODUCTION DESIGNER: DAN HORTON
WRITTEN BY: JEANNIE HUND AND MOLLY WIGAND
ILLUSTRATIONS BY: JACK PULLAN

ISBN: 978-1-63059-888-4
BOK1047

MADE IN CHINA
0817

GRAND OLOGY

THE A–Z Guide for Grandmas

BY MEEMAW JEANNIE AND GRANDMA MOLLY

WELCOME TO BEING

GRAND!

JUST WHEN YOU THINK YOU'VE SEEN IT ALL, YOUR WORLD IS TURNED UPSIDE DOWN, YOUR PRIORITIES REARRANGE, YOUR ATTITUDE IS GIVEN AN EXTREME MAKEOVER, AND YOUR HEART IS UTTERLY POSSESSED BY AN ADORABLE, MIRACULOUS, IRRESISTIBLE CREATURE—YOUR GRANDBABY!

IT'S A NEW, WONDERFUL WORLD, BEING GRAND, AND YOU'RE GONNA LOVE IT HERE. BUT, BE WARNED, YOU'LL NEVER BE THE SAME. (NOR WILL YOU WANT TO BE.) A WHOLE NEW KIND OF LOVE, FUN, AND MISCHIEF ARE REDEFINING YOUR LIFE. HERE'S A LITTLE GUIDEBOOK ON EVERYTHING FROM A TO Z TO HELP GET YOU STARTED.

"HAVE FUN! SPOIL 'EM ROTTEN! AND NEVER LOOK BACK!" —MEEMAW JEANNIE

A+++:

THE GRADE GRANDMA GIVES HER GRANDCHILDREN
FOR BEING SO DARNED CUTE AND LOVABLE.

AGAPE:

THAT TRULY SELFLESS, WONDROUS
"GRANDMOTHER" KIND OF LOVE YOU
CANNOT HELP BUT FEEL FOR YOUR GRANDBABIES.

AHHH:

Sound Grandma makes when putting her feet up after a long, fun day with the grandkids.

ANNIE:

Broadway play from which Mimi happily performs beloved show tunes for her grandbabies. See also: CHICAGO and MY FAIR LADY.

AWWW:

Often-used expression of being utterly gobsmacked by each sweet, adorable thing her grandchild does.

APPLESAUCE:

What you turn into when you hear your grandchild first say, "Love you."

ATTITUDE:

Part of a kid that made you tear your hair out as a mom but is cute and funny when you get to be a grandma.

THE DIFFERENCE BETWEEN PARENTS AND GRANDMAS:

Parents...	Grandmas...
Are mortified by child's tantrums in public spaces.	Dare judgmental passersby to comment at own risk.
Strictly enforce "time-out."	Say "Time-out from time-out. Come to Grandma!"
Read baby books and Web M.D. for guidance	Pretty much just wingin' it.
Loves those kids!	Ditto!

BIFOCALS:

Expensive "toys" attached to a grandma's face until a grandchild grabs them and mangles the titanium frames beyond recognition.

BLACKMAIL:

Controlling your kids by threatening to tell the grandchildren the dumb things their parents did when they were young.

BOSS OF YOU:

WHAT YOUR GRANDCHILD IS. SEE ALSO: "WHAT YOUR GRANDCHILD'S PARENTS AREN'T."

BOTTLE:

WHAT BABY DRINKS FROM. ALSO WHAT GRANDMA DRINKS FROM AFTER THE GRANDKIDS LEAVE.

BUZZKILL:

WHAT HAPPENS WHEN WELL-INTENDED, OVEREAGER PARENTS COME HOME EARLY AND INTERRUPT GRANDMA'S PLAYDATE WITH THE GRANDKIDS.

Instructions for baby's bottle	Instructions for grandma's bottle
Carefully mix formula. Measure twice!	Eyeball it. An extra splash can't hurt.
Test temperature on inner arm.	Grab some ice and shake it up, baby.
Easy does it!	Down the hatch!
Nitey Nite.	Nitey Nite.

CAR SEAT:
Essential safety device, the mastery of which requires a PhD in quantum mechanics.

CELL PHONE:
Expensive device for storing and sharing grandkid photos.

CHILDPROOFING:
Ingenious system of locks, latches, and levers designed to keep Grandma out of her own junk drawer.

COOKIES:

1) THE MOST ESSENTIAL BUILDING BLOCK OF NANA'S FIVE BASIC FOOD GROUPS.

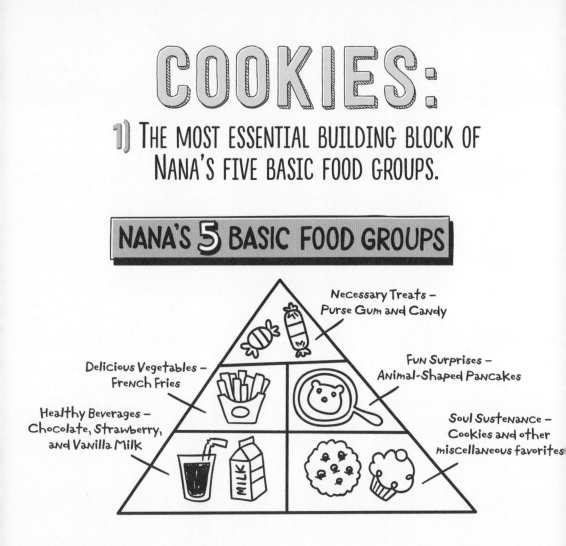

NANA'S 5 BASIC FOOD GROUPS

Necessary Treats –
Purse Gum and Candy

Fun Surprises –
Animal-Shaped Pancakes

Delicious Vegetables –
French Fries

Healthy Beverages –
Chocolate, Strawberry,
and Vanilla Milk

Soul Sustenance –
Cookies and other
miscellaneous favorites

2) The foundation for a grandchild's Zen-like contentment, rock solid self-esteem, and lifelong satisfaction.

3) A tonic with the power to improve a host of conditions, such as hunger, boredom, disappointment, loneliness, frustration, homework overload, ouchies, and every manner of existential crisis.

CUTE:

What other people's grandkids aren't, compared to yours. Sorry. They just aren't.

DELIVERY:

THE PROCESS BY WHICH YOUR GRANDCHILD ARRIVES AND MAKES YOUR LIFE COMPLETE ALL OVER AGAIN.

DOOFUS:

WHAT A NEW GRANDMA FEELS LIKE WHEN SHE PUTS THE DIAPER ON BACKWARDS AND CAN'T FIND THE STICKY TABS. (BUT DON'T FRET. IT HAPPENS TO US ALL.)

DREAMS:

WHAT MEEMAW WANTS TO MAKE COME TRUE FOR HER GRANDCHILDREN ON BIRTHDAYS, CHRISTMASES, AND ALL THE DAYS IN BETWEEN.

DRUM SET:

THE PERFECT GET-EVEN GIFT FOR YOUR GRANDKIDS' PARENTS. SEE ALSO: PLAY-DOH AND HAMSTER.

EARLY:

When morning comes after a fussy night with the grandbaby. See also: OMG so early.

ECSTATIC:

Expression on Gigi's face first time her grandbaby says, "GIGI."

ELDERLY:

WHAT YOUR GRANDPARENTS WERE.

ETERNALLY YOUNG AND AWESOME:

WHAT YOU ARE.

FIRSTS:

MILESTONES OF GRANDPARENTHOOD, INCLUDING FIRST DIAPER BLOWOUT, FIRST DROOLY KISS, AND FIRST "LET'S NOT TELL MOM" MOMENT.

ARE YOU A FUN GRANDMA?
TAKE THIS QUIZ AND SEE!

	YES	NO
Do you, at all times, have bubble gum in your purse?	☐	☐
Have you recently uttered the words, "Let's not tell Mom"?	☐	☐
Is your residence basically a toy store in a house disguise?	☐	☐
Does your car stereo blare silly songs, even when you're alone?	☐	☐
Do you allow finger painting and pot-and-pan parades?	☐	☐

FUN GRANDMA:

What you want to be, despite your son's/daughter's best efforts to make you the Boring and Obedient Grandma.

Score 1 point for each "YES."

5 points	Off-the-charts wacky Grandma!
4 points	Grandkids' dream come true!
3 points	More fun than the average Meemaw!
2 points	Favorite grown-up of at least one little person!
1 point	You're a laugh and a half!
0 points	No worries! You make your own brand of Grandma fun!

GAME:

What Meemaw can make out of absolutely anything, because she is a **MAGICAL, FUN-MAKING GENIUS.**

GARAGE SALES:

A TREASURE TROVE OF CHILD-PLEASING BARGAINS DEEMED UNSUITABLE BY YOUR GRANDCHILD'S PARENTS.

GRANDFATHER:

WELL-MEANING PARTNER IN GRANDPARENTHOOD WHO GOES MISSING AT THE FIRST SIGN OF A DIAPER BLOWOUT.

GUN:

WHAT YOUR GRANDCHILD WILL TURN EVERY STICK, HAIRBRUSH, OR GRILLED CHEESE SANDWICH INTO, REGARDLESS OF A FAMILY'S POLITICAL BELIEFS.

"HAVE FUN!":

GRANNY'S **ONE** RULE. THERE IS NO WIGGLE ROOM WHEN IT COMES TO OBEYING IT. ENFORCEMENT IS STRICT!

HEAVY:

WHAT PARENTS ARE. ALSO WHAT NANA IS NOT. EXAMPLE: I GUESS I HAVE TO BE **"THE HEAVY"** HERE AND INSIST ON VEGETABLES BEFORE ICE CREAM.

HOOEY:

Mimi's umbrella term for
"the latest child-rearing techniques."
See also: sleep-training, "cry it out,"
co-sleeping, and baby-led weaning.

HOKEY POKEY:

Classic dance for which your grandkids
are already too cool at birth.

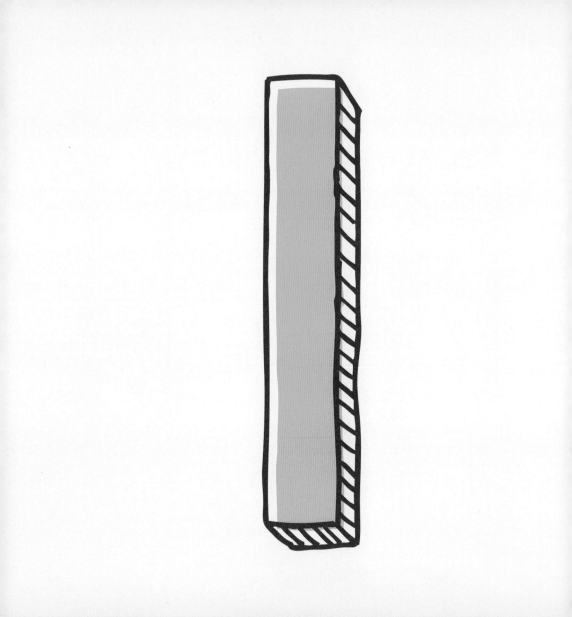

INSTRUCTIONS:

WHAT THE GRANDKIDS' MOMS LEAVE YOU PAGES OF AS IF YOU'VE NEVER DONE THIS BEFORE. INSTRUCTIONS MAKE LOVELY DROP CLOTHS FOR THE HIGH CHAIR.

What Mom Says	What Grandma Hears
No cookies.	Yes cookies.
Tummy time.	Cookie time.
Sleep training.	Cookie training.

JAMMIES:

WHAT GRAMMAS LET GRANDKIDS WEAR ALL DAY IF THEY WANT TO.

JEALOUSY:

WHAT PARENTS SOMETIMES FEEL WHEN THEIR KIDS LOVE THEIR GRANDMAS. SO TRY TO HAVE THEM LOVE YOU BUT NOT TOO MUCH. HEY, THAT'S TOO MUCH. OK, YOU'RE GOOD.

JEWELRY:

Irresistible item Baby yanks through Grandma's earlobe or off her neck and then mistakes for a snack.

KNICKKNACKS:

Adorable decorative items that small children must destroy. Put them up. For ten years. Seriously.

KNOW-IT-ALL:

Well, obviously, that's you. But try not to act like it.

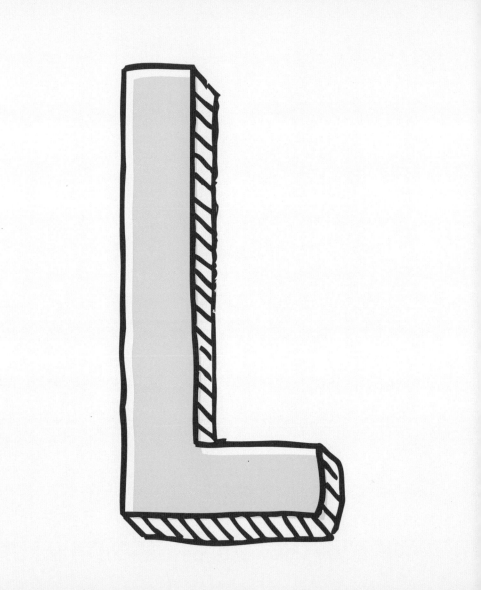

LABOR:

The only thing more painful than being bonked in the nose by your grandbaby's head.

LOVEY:

Baby's favorite blanket or cuddly toy. Grandma's NO. 1 RIVAL.

LULLABIES:

Soothing songs Grandma sings to baby, mostly Motown, and there's not a darn thing baby can do about it.

MAMA:

THE ONE AND ONLY SOLUTION TO SOME OF A GRANDBABY'S PROBLEMS. AS IT SHOULD BE.

MARKERS, PERMANENT:

THE CHOICE OF CHOOSY GRANDKID PICASSOS ADORNING GRANDMA'S WALLS AND FURNITURE.

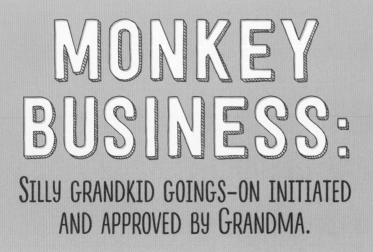

MELT:
WHAT HAPPENS TO GRANDMA'S HEART EVERY TIME SHE SEES HER GRANDBABY.

MONKEY BUSINESS:
SILLY GRANDKID GOINGS-ON INITIATED AND APPROVED BY GRANDMA.

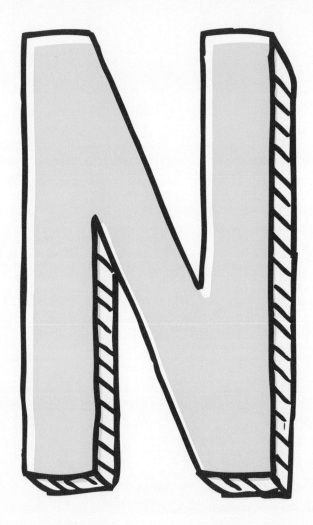

NOT ALLOWED:

THE MOST HILARIOUS TWO-WORD PHRASE NANNY CAN POSSIBLY HEAR COMING FROM THE LIPS OF GRANDBABY'S PARENTS. OFTEN LEADS TO PRIVATE FITS OF LAUGHTER AND COVERT, SUBVERSIVE ACTIVITIES.

NOTHING:

WHAT YOUR GRANDCHILD'S PARENTS THINK YOU KNOW ABOUT RAISING KIDS UNTIL IT'S THE MIDDLE OF THE NIGHT AND THEY'RE OUT OF IDEAS.

OFF-THE-WALL:

How your childcare methods sound to your kids. Also, where the grandkids bounce whenever Nana is near.

OK:

What everything that was OK for parents to do thirty years ago isn't anymore, like putting a baby on his front. No, back. Wait, front. This is so confusing. Also, let them cry it out. No, don't. Pick them up. But you'll spoil them. Sigh . . .

PACIFIER:

1.) AN OLD-TIMEY WORD FOR A PRICELESS, BELOVED, SUCKABLE OBJECT THAT PARENTS AND GRANDPARENTS *ALL* AGREE TO EMBRACE BECAUSE IT MAKES BABY SO DOGGONE HAPPY.

2.) A BOGUS PHRASE SUCH AS "YES, I'LL BE SURE SHE NAPS RIGHT ON SCHEDULE," AND "NO POPSICLES FOR BABY," UTTERED TO KEEP NEW PARENTS FROM BUGGING THE HELL OUT OF GRANNY.

PETS:

Supposed grandchild playthings. Teeth, claws, and grabby little fists. What could possibly go wrong?

POOP:

Fun word to teach toddler grandchildren to say just before they go home. See also: Fart.

PROFANITY:

Grandma's favorite vocabulary words, replaced by "BULL SUGAR," "FUDGE IT," AND "ASH BOWL" when in the company of impressionable grandchildren.

P&Q:

PEACE AND QUIET—TWO THINGS YOU THINK YOU HAVE TOO MUCH OF UNTIL YOU WATCH THE GRANDKIDS FOR A DAY.

QUIT:

WHAT YOUR **NANA-SIZED LOVE** WILL NEVER DO, NO MATTER WHAT.

RAISINS:

Orifice-friendly items that should be purged from the premises before young grandchildren visit. See also: Peas, Jelly beans, and Gravel.

REINVENTING THE WHEEL:

See twenty-first century parenting.

R&R:

1). Pre-grandbaby definition:
ROCK & ROLL;

2.) Current definition:
REST & REJUVENATION.

RULES:

Things to keep in mind when dealing with those pesky intermediaries known as the grandbaby's parents.

SCARF:

Essential fashion accessory that adds panache to a silk camisole while hiding the spit-up stain.

SCHEDULE:

A BUNCH OF UNIMPORTANT CRAP, CARVED IN STONE, WHICH GRANDMA BLISSFULLY IGNORES.

SNOT:

STICKY ELIXIR OF RESPIRATORY COOTIES WIPED ON GRANDMA'S FAVORITE SWEATER. **SEE ALSO: SPIT-UP.**

SPOIL:

A CRUDE, RUDE, ARCHAIC WORD CREATED BY FUN-HATERS, WHICH HAS NO APPLICATION WHATSOEVER TO HOW GRANDMA CHOOSES TO TREAT HER GRANDBABY.

STRANGER:

A PERSON WHO HAS NOT YET SEEN
PHOTOS OF THE GRANDKIDS.

STROLLER:

Grandchild's sweet ride. Equipped with cup holders, Bluetooth, and sunroof, it costs more than Grandma's first car.

SUGAR:

Gramma's very favorite thing and not only when she's baking. EXAMPLE: GIVE GRAMMA SOME SUGAR.

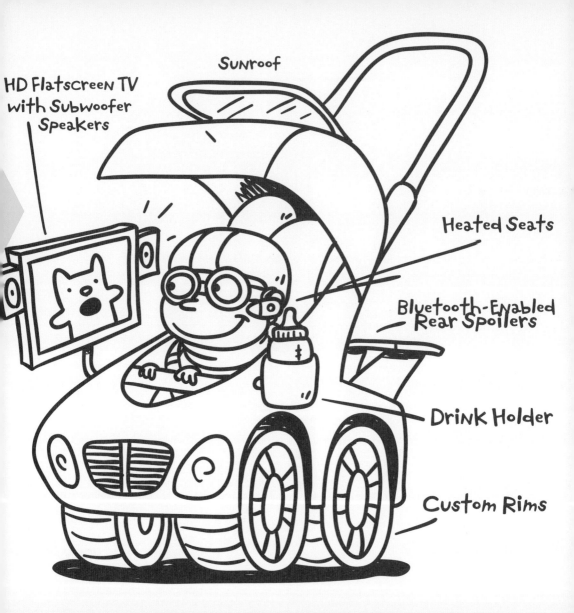

TECHNOLOGY:

Electronic mysteries magically decoded through the placenta, enabling toddlers to program Grandma's remote.

TOILET TRAINING:

Stressful time *during* which Grandma should keep her mouth shut and *after* which babysitting is much more fun.

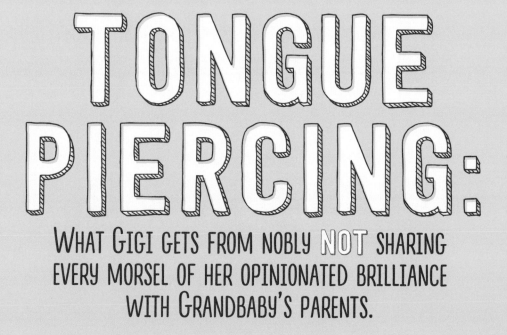

TONGUE PIERCING:

WHAT GIGI GETS FROM NOBLY **NOT** SHARING EVERY MORSEL OF HER OPINIONATED BRILLIANCE WITH GRANDBABY'S PARENTS.

TV:

A POWERFUL SOOTHING DEVICE USED
TO BRING A GRANNY AND GRANDKID SOME
WELL-DESERVED R&R, KNOWN FOR
INDUCING A HEALING, TRANCE-LIKE STATE.

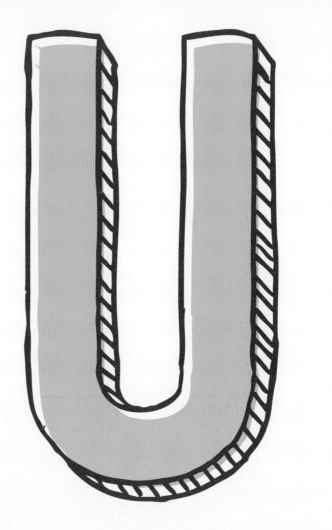

UGLY CRY:

THAT THING THAT HAPPENS WHEN YOU
DESPERATELY MISS THE LITTLE DARLINGS
AND THEY'RE MILES AWAY.

UNDER LOCK AND KEY:

WHERE GRANDMA KEEPS THE GOOD CHOCOLATE WHEN THE LITTLE ONES VISIT.

UPSIDE DOWN:

WHERE YOU'LL HAVE TO TURN YOUR WHOLE HOUSE LOOKING FOR THE REMOTE AFTER THE GRANDKIDS LEAVE.

UTERUS:

THAT PLACE WHERE BOTH GRANDMA'S KIDS AND HER GRANDKIDS WERE A LOT EASIER TO HANDLE.

VAPORIZER:

MAGICAL DEVICE THAT EASES A GRANDCHILD'S RESPIRATORY ISSUES WHILE REMOVING WALLPAPER.

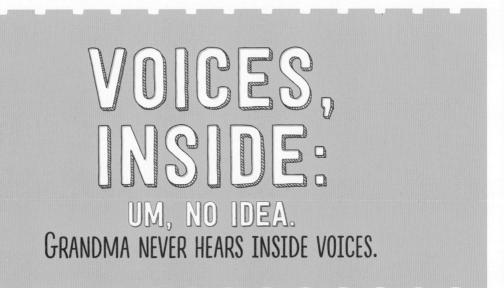

VOICES, INSIDE:

UM, NO IDEA.
GRANDMA NEVER HEARS INSIDE VOICES.

WEIGHT:

THAT THING YOU THINK YOU'LL LOSE BY RUNNING AROUND AFTER YOUR GRANDCHILDREN BUT ACTUALLY YOU JUST GAIN FROM ALL THE POP-TARTS.

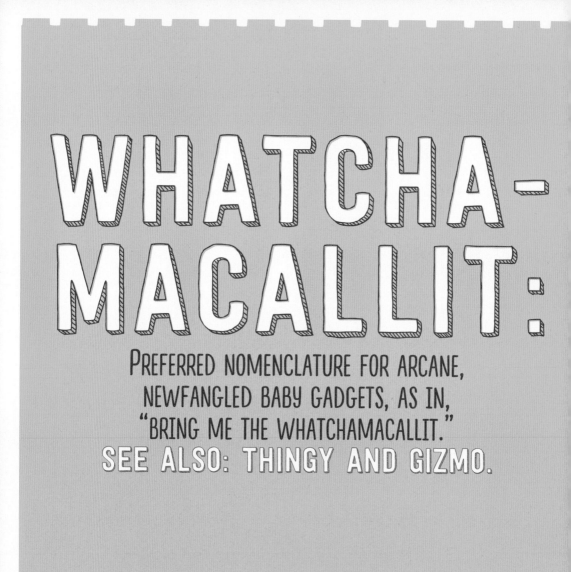

WHATCHA-MACALLIT:

Preferred nomenclature for arcane, newfangled baby gadgets, as in, "bring me the whatchamacallit."
See also: thingy and gizmo.

WHOOPEE CUSHION:

One of many lowbrow toys introduced by grandparents, reviled by mom, and adored by grandkids.

Xs AND Os:

SOMETHING GRANDMAS AND GRANDKIDS ARE
GUARANTEED A LIFETIME SUPPLY OF!

XXXXXL:

THE SIZE OF YOUR NANA LOVE.

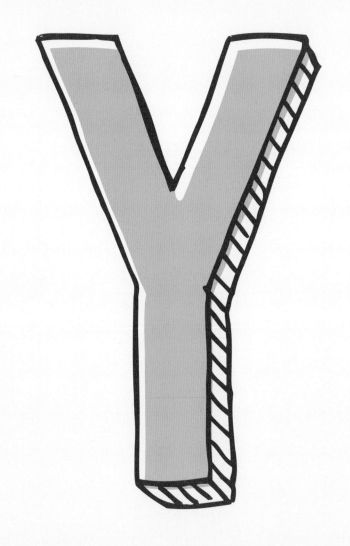

YAWN:

GRANDBABY'S BOGUS SIGNAL OF FATIGUE.
GET READY FOR THREE HOURS OF WALKING THE
FLOOR WHISPER-SINGING "B-I-N-G-O."

"YOU WERE RIGHT, MOM.":

THREE WORDS YOU WILL HEAR WHEN YOUR GRANDCHILD
REACHES THE MOUTHY HELL THAT IS PUBERTY.
SEE ALSO: "TOLD YOU SO," WHICH IS HOW YOU RESPOND.

ZEBRA:

STILL THE LAST ANIMAL IN AN ALPHABET BOOK,
SO AT LEAST **THAT** HASN'T CHANGED.

ZOOM IN:

THE ONLY WAY TO FULLY CAPTURE THE INCOMPARABLE
CUTENESS OF YOUR GRANDKID'S FACE.

AND ALWAYS REMEMBER:

No matter what style of grand you are...old-fashioned, newfangled, urban, rural, career-goddess, homebody, world-traveler, fashionista, artsy-craftsy, biker-babe, or pure Zen...

...and no matter what name you go by...

GRANDMA, GIGI, MEEMAW, ABUELA, NANA, YA YA, GLAMMA, BOO BAH, GRANDMOTHER, OR MIMI...

THERE IS ONE PLACE WHERE YOU WERE DESIGNED TO FIT PERFECTLY JUST AS YOU ARE—

IF YOU HAVE ENJOYED THIS BOOK
OR IT HAS TOUCHED YOUR LIFE IN SOME WAY,
WE WOULD LOVE TO HEAR FROM YOU.

PLEASE SEND COMMENTS TO:
HALLMARK BOOK FEEDBACK
P.O. BOX 419034
MAIL DROP 100
KANSAS CITY, MO 64141

OR EMAIL US AT:

BOOKNOTES@HALLMARK.COM